Unveiling the Ir

A Journey Beyond Language

Contents

Unveiling the Ineffable:
A Journey Beyond Language

We will:

Introduce the concept of the ineffable and its significance in human experience.

Explain how the book aims to explore the boundaries of language and delve into the realm of the unexplainable.

Set the stage for a captivating exploration of the ineffable.

Chapter 1: The Power and Limitations of Language

Discuss the evolution of language and its role in human communication.

Explore the strengths and weaknesses of language in expressing complex emotions, abstract concepts, and transcendental experiences.

Introduce the idea that some experiences are beyond the grasp of words.

Chapter 2: The Ineffable in Nature

Highlight moments in nature that elicit a sense of awe and wonder.

Describe experiences such as witnessing a breathtaking sunset, encountering the vastness of the ocean, or being immersed in the beauty of a starry night.

Reflect on the difficulty of capturing these experiences accurately through language.

Chapter 3: Mystical and Spiritual Dimensions

Explore the ineffable aspects of mystical and spiritual experiences across cultures.

Discuss encounters with the divine, transcendental meditation, or mystical states of consciousness.

Examine how individuals struggle to convey these experiences and the significance they hold in shaping their lives.

Chapter 4: Artistic Expressions Beyond Words

Delve into the realm of art, music, and dance as avenues to express the ineffable.

Explore the works of artists who strive to capture the unexplainable in their creations.

Analyze how art forms can evoke emotions, provoke thought, and touch the deepest parts of the human experience.

Chapter 5: Love and Intimacy

Investigate the complexities of love and intimacy, which often defy language's ability to fully capture their essence.

Discuss the emotional depths, profound connections, and transformative power of love.

Examine the challenges of describing love and its impact on personal growth.

Chapter 6: Scientific and Philosophical Perspectives

Present scientific and philosophical viewpoints on the limits of language and the ineffable.

Explore theories of quantum mechanics, consciousness, and the nature of reality.

Discuss the inherent challenges faced by scientists and philosophers in articulating the inexplicable.

Chapter 7: Embracing the Ineffable

Encourage readers to embrace the ineffable and find solace in the limitations of language.

Provide suggestions on how to cultivate a deeper connection with the unexplainable aspects of life.

Highlight the importance of mindfulness, openness, and embracing the unknown.

The conclusion will:

Recap the exploration of the ineffable and its multifaceted manifestations.

Encourage readers to embrace the mystery and wonder that exist beyond the confines of language.

Inspire a sense of awe, curiosity, and appreciation for the profound experiences that cannot be easily explained with words.

Introduction:

The concept of the ineffable revolves around experiences and aspects of life that are challenging or impossible to express in words. It recognizes that there are certain feelings, moments, or phenomena that go beyond what language can adequately convey. Exploring the ineffable allows us to appreciate the limitations of language and embrace the mysterious and profound aspects of human experience.

Parable 1: The Magic Butterfly Once upon a time, in a beautiful garden, there lived a group of children who loved to play and explore. One sunny day, as they were chasing butterflies, they came across a butterfly unlike any they had ever seen before. It shimmered with a magical glow and seemed to dance on the air. The children were captivated by its beauty and tried to describe it to each other using words. But no matter how hard they tried, they couldn't capture the true essence of its magnificence. They realized that the magic of the butterfly was ineffable, something that could only be felt and experienced in the heart.

Parable 2: The Song of the Stars On a clear night, a young child named Maya lay on a grassy field, gazing up at the sky. As she looked at the countless stars twinkling above her, she felt a deep sense of wonder and awe. She tried to tell her friend about the beauty she saw, but her words fell short. So instead, Maya closed her eyes and listened with her heart. In that quiet moment, she heard the stars singing a melodic symphony that resonated deep within her soul. It was a song that no words could capture, a song that could only be heard in the silence of one's spirit. Maya realized that the song of the stars was ineffable, something that went beyond language and touched the deepest part of her being.

Parable 3: The Puzzle of Emotions In a small village, there lived a wise old storyteller named Ben. One day, a curious child named Alex approached Ben and asked, "Why are some feelings hard to explain?" Ben smiled and replied, "Imagine you have a puzzle with many pieces. Some feelings are like those puzzle pieces. They don't fit neatly into words, and trying to force them can make us feel frustrated. Instead, we can learn to appreciate the mystery of those emotions and let them be, just like we enjoy the beauty of a puzzle coming together without fully understanding how."

Through these parables, children can begin to understand that there are experiences and feelings that transcend the limits of language. They can learn to appreciate the beauty and mystery of these ineffable moments, recognizing that sometimes the most profound things in life are those that cannot be fully explained with words.

The book "Unveiling the Ineffable: A Journey Beyond Language" invites readers, including children, to embark on a captivating exploration of the boundaries of language and the realm of the unexplainable. It aims to foster curiosity and open minds to the wonder and mystery that exist beyond the confines of words.

Through stories and parables, children can begin to grasp the concept of the ineffable and its significance in human experience.

Parable 1: The Rainbow of Feelings Once upon a time, in a colorful village, there lived a group of children who loved to express their feelings through drawings. One day, they gathered in a meadow and started to draw rainbows. Each child used different colors to represent their emotions. One drew a vibrant red for excitement, another a calm blue for peacefulness, and yet another a sunny yellow for happiness. But there were some feelings that couldn't be captured by any single color. They were like the magical hues that appeared between the colors of the rainbow. The children realized that these feelings were ineffable, too complex and beautiful to be described with just one color. They embraced the mystery and celebrated the joy of experiencing emotions that words couldn't fully express.

Parable 2: The Secret Language of Trees In a lush forest, a curious child named Lily spent her days exploring and talking to the trees. She noticed that each tree had a unique personality, whispering secrets and stories in a language only they understood. Lily yearned to know their language, but the trees couldn't convey it with words. One day, as Lily sat beneath an ancient oak, she closed her eyes and listened deeply. In the stillness of the forest, the trees shared their wisdom through rustling leaves, gentle creaks, and the sway of branches. Lily realized that the language of trees was ineffable, a language of connection and harmony that couldn't be spoken but could be felt in the core of her being.

Parable 3: The Magic of Imagination In a world where dreams came alive, a young child named Max had a special gift - a vivid imagination. Max's imagination was like a door to infinite worlds and possibilities. When Max tried to describe these imaginative journeys, words fell short. One day, Max met an old storyteller who said, "Imagination is a magical realm beyond words. It's like a treasure map that guides you to undiscovered lands. The true power lies not in explaining every detail, but in embracing the wonder and letting your imagination soar." Max understood that the magic of imagination was ineffable, a realm of endless enchantment that words alone couldn't capture.

Through these parables, children can grasp the idea that there are experiences, feelings, and realms that transcend the limitations of language. They learn to appreciate the beauty and mystery of the ineffable, cultivating a sense of wonder and curiosity that can enrich their understanding of themselves and the world around them.

Set amidst a world of wonders, the book "Unveiling the Ineffable: A Journey Beyond Language" invites children on a captivating exploration of the ineffable. It opens the door to a realm where words fall short, encouraging young readers to embrace the mystery and beauty that lies beyond what can be easily explained. Through stories and parables, children can embark on a magical journey, discovering the enchantment of the ineffable.

Parable 1: The Whispering Breeze In a peaceful meadow, a young girl named Ella loved to listen to the breeze as it gently rustled through the tall grass. One day, while lying on her back and gazing at the clouds, Ella closed her eyes and let the breeze caress her face. She felt a sense of calm and wonder washing over her, as if the breeze was whispering secrets only her heart could hear. When she tried to describe the feeling to her friends, the words slipped away. Ella realized that the language of the breeze was ineffable, a language of tranquility and serenity that could only be felt, not spoken.

Parable 2: The Dance of Fireflies In a magical forest, a young boy named Oliver loved to chase fireflies. As the sun set and darkness embraced the land, the forest came alive with tiny flickering lights. Oliver would run after them, laughing and reaching out his hand, trying to catch their fleeting glow. One night, as he watched the fireflies dance around him, he noticed that their beauty transcended words. They weaved patterns of light and mystery, enchanting his senses. Oliver realized that the dance of fireflies was ineffable, a symphony of illumination that evoked awe and wonder, impossible to capture with language alone.

Parable 3: The Silent Friendship In a small village, there lived a child named Mia who discovered a silent friendship with a wise old turtle named Oscar. Every day, Mia would visit Oscar by the tranquil pond and share stories with him, even though the turtle couldn't speak in words. Instead, Oscar communicated through his gentle presence, his wise eyes, and the serenity of his being. Mia realized that their connection was ineffable, a friendship that surpassed the need for words. It was a deep understanding that unfolded in the stillness, where silence spoke volumes.

Through these parables, children can begin to grasp the concept of the ineffable, the experiences and phenomena that elude easy explanation. They learn to appreciate the beauty and magic of the unexplainable, understanding that sometimes the most profound things in life are those that can't be fully captured with words. This exploration of the ineffable opens their hearts and minds to the vast mysteries of the world, nurturing a sense of wonder and curiosity that can enrich their lives.

Chapter 1: The Power and Limitations of Language

Introduction: Language is a remarkable tool that allows us to communicate, express our thoughts, and share our experiences. However, it also has its limitations when it comes to capturing the full breadth of human experience. In this chapter, we will explore the power and limitations of language, and how it relates to the concept of the ineffable.

Parable 1: The Melody of Words In a bustling town, there lived a young girl named Lily who loved to sing. Her voice could fill the air with beautiful melodies, touching the hearts of those who listened. One day, Lily tried to describe the feeling of music to her friend, Emma, who had never heard it before. Lily searched for words to explain how music made her feel alive, but the words seemed to fall short. Instead, she invited Emma to close her eyes and listen to a song. As the melody swept through the room, Emma's heart danced to the rhythm, and she understood that the true magic of music was ineffable. It was a language that transcended words, speaking directly to the soul.

Parable 2: The Paintbrush of Emotions In an art studio, a young painter named Alex loved to express emotions through colors and brushstrokes. Each painting was a window into Alex's heart, capturing the complexities of joy, sadness, and love. One day, a friend asked Alex to describe the emotions behind a particular painting. Alex struggled to find the right words to convey the depth and intricacy of feelings. Instead, he handed his friend a paintbrush and a blank canvas. As his friend dipped the brush into different colors and let emotions guide the strokes, he realized that the true essence of Alex's painting was ineffable. It was a language of colors, shapes, and textures that resonated with emotions in a way that words couldn't fully capture.

Parable 3: The Hidden Language of Smiles In a vibrant community, a child named Max loved to explore the world with a smile on his face. Max discovered that smiles had a special power—they could convey joy, comfort, and kindness without uttering a word. One day, Max met a new friend, Sarah, who spoke a different language. Despite the language barrier, Max and Sarah found a way to connect through their smiles. Their shared laughter and warmth created a bond that surpassed the need for words. Max realized that the language of smiles was ineffable, a universal expression of happiness and friendship that could bridge any linguistic divide.

Through these parables, children can begin to understand the power of language in conveying ideas and emotions, while also recognizing its limitations. They learn that some experiences and feelings are best understood through alternative means, such as music, art, or nonverbal communication. By exploring the boundaries of language, children can develop a deeper appreciation for the vastness and complexity of human experience beyond what words alone can convey.

Chapter 2: Delving into the Realm of the Unexplainable
Introduction: In this chapter, we will venture into the realm of the unexplainable, where words fall short and the mysteries of life unfold. We will explore experiences and phenomena that defy simple explanations,

embracing the beauty and wonder found in the ineffable.

Parable 1: The Starry Night's Tale In a small village nestled beneath a vast sky, there lived a young dreamer named Sofia. One clear night, Sofia gazed up at the stars, feeling a sense of awe and wonder. She tried to fathom the vastness of the universe, the countless galaxies twinkling above her. As she shared her thoughts with her wise grandmother, Sofia realized that the stars held a story beyond the reach of words. Her grandmother smiled and told her a parable: "Imagine the stars as seeds of dreams. Each one carries the hopes and aspirations of countless beings across the cosmos. Their story is written in the constellations, connecting us to the vastness of the unknown. Embrace the mystery, Sofia, and let the beauty of the starry night speak to your heart." Sofia understood that the true magic of the stars was ineffable, a cosmic tale that transcended words and ignited the imagination.

Parable 2: The Enchanted Forest's Whispers. Deep within an ancient forest, a young adventurer named Ethan wandered among the towering trees and vibrant foliage. The forest emanated a sense of magic and secrets waiting to be discovered. As Ethan explored, he noticed how the rustling leaves and murmurs of the forest seemed to communicate with one another. Curious, he sought the guidance of a wise old owl. The owl shared a parable: "In this enchanted forest, the language spoken is one of whispers and hidden meanings. The trees and creatures communicate through their very presence, sharing wisdom and unity that cannot be confined to words. Open your heart, Ethan, and listen to the forest's symphony. There, you will discover the profound beauty of the ineffable." Inspired, Ethan embraced the silence, allowing the forest's whispers to guide him on a journey of discovery beyond the limits of language.

Parable 3: The Riddle of Serendipity In a bustling city, a young seeker named Maya found herself pondering the nature of serendipity—the delightful surprises and synchronicities that grace our lives. She sought answers from a wise old storyteller, who shared a parable: "Imagine life as a grand tapestry woven with threads of chance and destiny. Serendipity dances between those threads, revealing connections that go beyond words. It is the unexpected meeting, the fortuitous event that shapes our path. Embrace the riddle of serendipity, Maya, and trust in the magic of the unexplainable. The true meaning lies not in understanding it, but in appreciating the wonder it brings." Maya realized that the essence of serendipity was ineffable, a gentle nudge from the universe that eluded easy explanations but filled life with delightful surprises.

Through these parables, children can venture into the realm of the unexplainable, embracing the mysteries and wonders of life. They learn to appreciate the beauty found in experiences that go beyond words, and the profound lessons and connections that lie within the ineffable. By delving into the unexplainable, children can develop a sense of awe, curiosity, and reverence for the vast mysteries that surround us.

Chapter 3: Embracing the Ineffable in Everyday Life

Introduction: In this chapter, we will explore how the ineffable can be found in the ordinary moments of everyday life. We will discover that there is magic and beauty in the things we often overlook, and that by embracing the ineffable, we can find deeper meaning and appreciation for the world around us.

Parable 1: The Dance of Raindrops On a rainy day, a young girl named Lily stood by the window, watching the raindrops cascade down the glass. She marveled at how each droplet seemed to have a life of its own, falling from the sky and joining others in a delicate dance. Lily tried to explain the beauty of the rain to her friend, Jack, but found herself at a loss for words. Instead, she invited him outside and they stood under an umbrella, listening to the rhythmic pitter-patter of the rain. As they watched the dance of raindrops, they realized that the true magic of the rain was ineffable. It was a symphony of nature, a gentle reminder of the interconnectedness of all things, and a source of comfort and renewal that surpassed the limits of language.

Parable 2: The Warmth of a Hug In a cozy home, a little boy named Oliver often sought comfort in his mother's arms. Whenever he felt sad or scared, his mother would embrace him tightly, filling him with a sense of warmth and security. One day, Oliver's friend, Emily, asked him why hugs made him feel better. Oliver pondered the question and realized that the power of a hug was ineffable. It was a language of love, compassion, and reassurance that couldn't be fully explained in words. To help Emily understand, Oliver opened his arms and enveloped her in a warm embrace. In that moment, Emily felt the comfort and love that flowed through the ineffable language of a hug.

Parable 3: The Symphony of Silence In a peaceful garden, a young girl named Mia often sat on a bench, surrounded by blooming flowers and fluttering butterflies. As she observed the beauty of nature, she discovered the magic of silence. Mia noticed how the absence of words allowed her to be fully present in the moment, listening to the gentle whispers of the wind and the rustling of leaves. One day, her friend, Ethan, asked her what she found in the silence. Mia smiled and shared a parable: "Imagine silence as a symphony, Ethan. It is the space between notes, the pauses that give meaning to the music. In the silence, we can truly hear the world around us and connect with our inner selves. The symphony of silence is ineffable, a language that speaks volumes without uttering a word." Ethan closed his eyes and embraced the stillness, realizing the profound beauty and depth found in the ineffable language of silence.

Through these parables, children can learn to appreciate the beauty and magic in the ordinary moments of everyday life. They discover that there is a language beyond words, one that can be felt and experienced. By embracing the ineffable, children develop a deeper connection with themselves, others, and the world around them. They learn to treasure the small, seemingly insignificant moments that hold profound meaning and to approach life with a sense of wonder, curiosity, and gratitude.

Chapter 4: Seeking the Ineffable in Personal Growth and Relationships

Introduction: In this chapter, we will explore how the ineffable plays a role in our personal growth and relationships. We will delve into the transformative power of embracing the unexplainable, discovering that it can lead us to new insights, deeper connections, and a greater understanding of ourselves and others.

Parable 1: The Seed of Possibility In a humble garden, a young gardener named Anna carefully planted a tiny seed. She nurtured it with love, watered it with care, and watched as it sprouted into a beautiful plant. Anna marveled at the miracle of life and wanted to share her awe with her friend, Ben. She tried to describe the growth process of the seed but found it challenging to capture its essence in words. Instead, she handed him a seed and said, "Hold it gently, Ben, and imagine the possibilities contained within. This seed holds the ineffable magic of growth, transformation, and the boundless potential of life itself. As it unfolds, it teaches us to embrace the unknown and trust in the process of becoming." Ben embraced the seed, feeling a sense of wonder and recognizing that the true essence of growth was ineffable—a journey that transcended words and blossomed into something beautiful.

Parable 2: The Dance of Connection In a bustling city, a young dancer named Maya stepped onto the stage. As she moved and twirled, she felt a deep connection with the music, the audience, and her fellow dancers. Maya wanted to convey this profound sense of connection to her friend, Liam, who had never experienced dancing before. Unable to find the right words, she invited Liam to join her on the dance floor. As they swayed together, they felt a harmonious energy flowing between them— a language that went beyond spoken words. They realized that the true power of connection was ineffable. It was a dance of understanding, empathy, and shared experiences that could be felt in the depths of their hearts, far beyond what words could express.

Parable 3: The Mirror of Self-Reflection In a peaceful sanctuary, a young seeker named Emma sat in front of a mirror. She looked deeply into her own eyes, contemplating her thoughts, emotions, and dreams. Emma sought to understand herself better and longed to share her journey with her friend, Ethan. As she struggled to put her inner experiences into words, she handed Ethan a mirror and said, "Look closely, Ethan, and see the ineffable nature of self-reflection. The mirror reflects not only our physical appearance but also our thoughts, emotions, and the ever-changing landscape of our inner world. It reminds us that understanding ourselves is a lifelong journey, one that goes beyond the boundaries of language and requires deep introspection." Ethan held the mirror, seeing his own reflection and recognizing that the true beauty of self-reflection lay in the unexplainable depths of his own being.

Through these parables, children can embrace the role of the ineffable in their personal growth and relationships. They learn that there are aspects of life and human experience that cannot be easily explained or understood with words alone. By seeking the ineffable, children can embark on a journey of self-discovery, nurturing connections with others, and embracing the limitless possibilities of their own potential. They realize that the most profound moments of personal growth and connection often lie in the realm of the unexplainable, and by embracing it, they can cultivate a deeper sense of meaning, purpose, and fulfilment.

Chapter 5: Embracing the Mystery and Wonder of the Ineffable Universe
Introduction: In this chapter, we will explore how the ineffable manifests in the vastness of the universe and the mysteries that lie beyond our comprehension. We will embark on a cosmic journey, inviting children to embrace the awe-inspiring wonders of the world and find solace in the beauty of the unexplainable.

Parable 1: The Celestial Symphony In a quiet observatory, a young astronomer named Leo gazed at the night sky through a telescope. The stars and galaxies seemed to sing a celestial symphony, harmonizing in an intricate dance. Leo wanted to share the magnificence of the cosmos with his sister, Lily. He struggled to find words that could capture the grandeur of the universe. Instead, he guided Lily to a hilltop on a clear night. They lay down, their eyes fixed on the starlit sky. As they observed the shimmering constellations and heard the whispers of the universe, they realized that the true nature of the cosmos was ineffable. It was a symphony of light and energy, a cosmic tapestry that humbled the human spirit and invited contemplation of the mysteries that lie beyond our grasp.

Parable 2: The Dance of Time In a quiet library, a young scholar named Oliver pondered the nature of time. He delved into books, seeking answers to the enigma of past, present, and future. As he struggled to articulate his thoughts, he invited his friend, Mia, to join him. They sat in the library, surrounded by the vast collection of knowledge. Oliver shared a parable: "Imagine time as a flowing river, Mia. It carries us through the moments of our lives, each one unique and fleeting. But the true essence of time is ineffable—it cannot be grasped or defined. We can only embrace the dance of time, cherishing each passing moment and finding meaning in the present." Mia reflected on Oliver's words, realizing that the true wisdom of time lay in the acceptance of its mysteries, the appreciation of the now, and the fleeting beauty of each passing moment.

Parable 3: The Song of Existence In a serene meadow, a young philosopher named Sophia contemplated the nature of existence itself. She questioned the origins of life, the vastness of the cosmos, and the interconnectedness of all things. Sophia longed to share her philosophical musings with her friend, Ethan. She realized that words alone could not capture the depth of her thoughts. Instead, she led Ethan to a quiet spot where they sat under a mighty oak tree. They listened to the rustling leaves, the chirping birds, and the pulsating energy of life. In that moment of silence and observation, Sophia and Ethan felt a sense of unity with the universe. They understood that the true song of existence was ineffable—a symphony that echoed through all living beings, transcending the boundaries of language and inviting them to be a part of the cosmic dance.

Through these parables, children can embrace the mystery and wonder of the ineffable universe. They learn to gaze at the stars with awe, to ponder the nature of time, and to contemplate the vastness of existence. By accepting the limits of human understanding and finding solace in the unexplainable, children develop a sense of humility, curiosity, and reverence for the beauty and complexity of the world. They realize that the true joy lies not in unraveling all the mysteries but in embracing the eternal wonder that the ineffable universe offers.

Chapter 6: Embracing the Ineffable Within Ourselves

Introduction: In this final chapter, we will explore how the concept of the ineffable resides within each of us. We will delve into the depths of our own emotions, thoughts, and experiences, discovering the parts of ourselves that defy easy explanation. By embracing the ineffable within, children can cultivate self-acceptance, inner peace, and a deeper connection with their own essence.

Parable 1: The Kaleidoscope of Emotions In a colorful garden, a young girl named Maya found herself overwhelmed by a whirlwind of emotions. She felt joy, sadness, excitement, and fear all at once, struggling to understand and express what she was feeling. Maya sought the guidance of a wise butterfly who shared a parable: "Imagine your emotions as a kaleidoscope, Maya. They are a mosaic of colors, shifting and changing with each passing moment. Embrace the beauty of this kaleidoscope and allow yourself to feel without judgment. Some emotions are ineffable, transcending simple words. Trust that they are a part of your unique tapestry, guiding you on the journey of self-discovery."

Parable 2: The Silent Symphony of Thoughts In a quiet sanctuary, a young thinker named Ethan pondered the ceaseless stream of thoughts that filled his mind. Sometimes, he found it challenging to articulate his inner world and share his ideas with others. Ethan sought guidance from a wise owl who shared a parable: "Imagine your thoughts as a silent symphony, Ethan. They are the melodies that dance within your mind, shaping your perception of the world. Some thoughts may be difficult to express in words, and that's okay. Embrace the power of introspection and allow your thoughts to flow freely. Remember that the ineffable thoughts are as valuable as the ones you can put into words, for they hold insights that go beyond what language can convey."

Parable 3: The Inner Flame of Intuition In a serene forest, a young seeker named Lily embarked on a quest to find her inner guidance. She longed for clarity and direction in her life but often found herself at a loss for words when trying to explain her intuition. Lily sought counsel from a wise old tree who shared a parable: "Imagine your intuition as an inner flame, Lily. It flickers and glows, guiding you through the forest of life. Trust in its wisdom, even when it defies rational explanation. Embrace the ineffable nature of intuition, for it is a language that speaks directly to your soul. When you listen to its gentle whispers, you will find the answers you seek and navigate your path with grace."

Through these parables, children can embrace the ineffable within themselves. They learn that their emotions, thoughts, and intuition are a part of their unique tapestry of being. By accepting and honouring the aspects of themselves that cannot be easily explained, children can develop a deeper connection with their true essence. They learn to trust their intuition, listen to the symphony of their thoughts, and honor the kaleidoscope of their emotions. By embracing the ineffable within, children can cultivate self-acceptance, resilience, and a profound sense of inner peace.

Chapter 7: Living a Life Informed by the Ineffable

Introduction: In this final chapter, we will explore how the concept of the ineffable can guide us in living a meaningful and purposeful life. We will delve into the ways in which we can incorporate the wisdom of the unexplainable into our actions, relationships, and choices, ultimately leading to a more fulfilling existence.

Parable 1: The Whisper of Compassion In a bustling city, a young girl named Mia witnessed a scene of a stranger in need. She felt a tug in her heart, urging her to help, but she couldn't find the right words to explain her instinctual compassion. Mia sought guidance from a wise old woman who shared a parable: "Imagine compassion as a whisper, Mia. It is the gentle voice that guides us to extend kindness and empathy to others. Sometimes, the most powerful acts of compassion are those that cannot be explained in words. Embrace the ineffable nature of compassion, and let your actions speak louder than any language could convey."

Parable 2: The Tapestry of Connection In a vibrant community, a young boy named Oliver pondered the interconnectedness of all living beings. He marveled at the intricate web of relationships that shaped his life, yet struggled to put into words the depth of this interconnectedness. Oliver sought guidance from a wise elder who shared a parable: "Imagine connection as a tapestry, Oliver. Each thread represents a person, a moment, a shared experience. The true beauty of connection lies not in its explanations, but in the bonds that form and the love that flows between individuals. Embrace the ineffable nature of connection, and nurture the threads of love, kindness, and understanding that weave together the tapestry of life."

Parable 3: The Dance of Purpose In a serene garden, a young dreamer named Lily pondered her purpose in life. She yearned for a sense of direction and meaning, but couldn't quite put into words what she felt called to do. Lily sought guidance from a wise butterfly who shared a parable: "Imagine purpose as a dance, Lily. It is the rhythm that guides our steps, even when we cannot clearly articulate our destination. Embrace the ineffable nature of purpose and allow it to unfold naturally. Trust that the dance of purpose will lead you to the path that aligns with your truest self. Let go of the need for explicit explanations and surrender to the magic of the journey."

Through these parables, children can learn to live a life informed by the ineffable. They discover that there are aspects of our existence that cannot be easily explained or rationalized. By embracing the wisdom of the unexplainable, children can cultivate compassion, nurture connections, and discover their unique purpose. They learn to listen to the whispers of their hearts, honor the tapestry of relationships, and dance with purpose, even when the destination is unclear. By living a life informed by the ineffable, children can lead a more meaningful, authentic, and fulfilling existence.

Conclusion:
Throughout this book, we have embarked on a captivating exploration of the ineffable, the concept that eludes easy explanation through

words. We have journeyed through various realms, from the wonders of nature to the depths of our own being, from the mysteries of the universe to the connections we forge with others. In embracing the ineffable, children have learned to find solace in the unexplainable, to appreciate the beauty of the unknown, and to cultivate a sense of wonder and curiosity that will accompany them throughout their lives.

As a grand conclusion, here are nine additional parables that encapsulate the essence of the ineffable:

Parable 1: The Song of Laughter Imagine laughter as a symphony that fills the air, transcending language and bringing joy to all who hear it. The true essence of laughter is ineffable, a melody that unites hearts and uplifts spirits.

Parable 2: The Colors of Imagination Imagine imagination as a palette of vibrant colors, where ideas and dreams come to life. The true power of imagination lies in its ability to paint pictures that words alone cannot capture.

Parable 3: The Key of Curiosity Imagine curiosity as a magical key that unlocks the doors to new knowledge and understanding. The true nature of curiosity is ineffable, as it sparks a sense of wonder that propels us on a lifelong quest for discovery.

Parable 4: The Dance of Gratitude Imagine gratitude as a graceful dance, expressing appreciation for the simple joys and blessings in our lives. The true essence of gratitude is ineffable, as it fills our hearts with warmth and deepens our connection to the world around us.

Parable 5: The Whispers of Nature Imagine nature as a wise teacher, whispering its secrets through the rustling leaves, the babbling brooks, and the songs of birds. The true wisdom of nature is ineffable, as it reminds us of our interconnectedness with the Earth and the delicate balance of life.

Parable 6: The Puzzle of Friendship Imagine friendship as a beautiful puzzle, each piece representing a unique bond and shared experience. The true magic of friendship is ineffable, as it goes beyond words to create a sense of belonging and unconditional love.

Parable 7: The Path of Resilience Imagine resilience as a winding path that we traverse in the face of challenges and setbacks. The true nature of resilience is ineffable, as it empowers us to rise again, to learn and grow, and to find strength in the face of adversity.

Parable 8: The Joy of Serendipity Imagine serendipity as a delightful surprise that brings unexpected moments of joy and inspiration. The true joy of serendipity is ineffable, as it reminds us that life holds mysteries and treasures waiting to be discovered.

Parable 9: The Symphony of Love Imagine love as a symphony of emotions, a harmonious blend of compassion, kindness, and empathy. The true power of love is ineffable, as it transcends language and touches the depths of our souls.

Fun Games to Continue Exploring the Concept:

The Ineffable Charades: Take turns acting out emotions, experiences, or concepts that are difficult to explain with words. Encourage children to express these ideas through gestures and facial expressions, letting the other players guess the ineffable concept being portrayed.

Here are some examples of ineffable concepts that children can act out in The Ineffable Charades:

Concept: Serenity Description: Close your eyes, take a deep breath, and let your body relax. Move gracefully, with gentle and flowing gestures. Show a peaceful expression on your face, as if you are in a state of perfect calm and tranquility.

Concept: Euphoria Description: Jump up and down with excitement, throw your arms in the air, and wear a big, ecstatic smile. Show a burst of energy and convey a sense of overwhelming joy and happiness through your movements and expressions.

Concept: Confusion Description: Furrow your brow, tilt your head to the side, and gesture as if you're lost. Make puzzling facial expressions and use hand movements to convey a sense of being unsure or not understanding what is happening.

Concept: Inspiration Description: Stand tall, look up to the sky, and put your hand on your heart. Show a sense of wonder and awe on your face, as if you're being touched by something extraordinary. Use gestures to indicate that you are feeling inspired and motivated.

Concept: Anticipation Description: Tap your fingers on your chin, look around with excitement, and bounce lightly on your toes. Convey a sense of eager expectation and show that you are eagerly awaiting something exciting or important.

Concept: Nostalgia Description: Hold your hand to your heart, gaze into the distance with a wistful expression, and maybe even wipe away an imaginary tear. Show a longing for the past and use gestures to convey a sentimental and reminiscent mood.

Encourage children to use their body language, facial expressions, and gestures to express these ineffable concepts, while the other players try to guess what concept is being portrayed. This game can be a fun way for children to explore and understand emotions and experiences that are challenging to put into words.

Storytelling with the Ineffable: Have children create stories where the main characters encounter situations or feelings that cannot be easily explained with words. Encourage them to tap into their imagination and embrace the unexplainable in their narratives.

Here are some examples of storytelling prompts for children to embrace the ineffable in their stories:

Story Prompt: "The Enchanted Forest" Story Description: In a hidden corner of the world, there lies an enchanted forest where the trees whisper secrets and the animals possess magical abilities. Two friends stumble upon this mystical place and find themselves confronted with a dilemma that can only be solved by understanding the power of the ineffable.

Story Prompt: "The Time Traveler's Journal" Story Description: In the attic of an old house, a young adventurer discovers a journal filled with accounts of extraordinary experiences. Each entry details encounters with unexplainable phenomena and emotions beyond comprehension. As they read through the pages, the protagonist embarks on a journey to uncover the mysteries and learn the true nature of the ineffable.

Story Prompt: "The Forgotten Key" Story Description: In a dusty attic, a curious child discovers a rusty key hidden in an old chest. Little do they know, this key unlocks a hidden door that leads to a realm where the ineffable becomes tangible. Through their adventures, the protagonist learns valuable lessons about the beauty and complexity of life's unexplainable moments.

Story Prompt: "The Star Collector" Story Description: In a world where stars are physical entities that hold the essence of dreams and aspirations, a young stargazer sets out on a quest to collect the most radiant stars. Along the way, they encounter challenges that require them to navigate the unexplainable, learning that sometimes the greatest treasures are found in the intangible.

Story Prompt: "The Puzzle of Imagination" Story Description: In a small town, imagination suddenly disappears, leaving the residents devoid of inspiration and wonder. A group of adventurous children embarks on a quest to solve the puzzle of imagination and bring back the ineffable to their community. Through their journey, they discover that the power of storytelling and creativity can unlock the secrets of the unexplainable.

Encourage children to let their imagination soar and embrace the unexplainable in their storytelling. They can create characters, settings, and plotlines that incorporate magical elements, emotions, and experiences that go beyond words. Let their stories explore the depth and wonder of the ineffable.

The Ineffable Art Challenge: Provide children with art supplies and ask them to create visual representations of ineffable concepts such as love, happiness, or the beauty of nature. Encourage them to use colors, shapes, and textures to convey the unexplainable essence of these concepts.

Here are some examples of visual representations of ineffable concepts that children can create for The Ineffable Art Challenge:

Concept: Love Artwork Description: Using vibrant reds and pinks, create a heart-shaped collage with different textures and materials. Incorporate images or symbols that represent love, such as doves or intertwined hands.

Concept: Happiness Artwork Description: Paint a colorful abstract piece using bright yellows, oranges, and blues. Use bold brushstrokes and add splashes of glitter or confetti to represent the joyful and radiant nature of happiness.

Concept: Beauty of Nature Artwork Description: Create a mixed-media piece inspired by nature's beauty. Use natural materials like leaves, flowers, and twigs to create a textured collage. Paint a scenic background with lush greens, serene blues, and vibrant blooms.

Concept: Wonder Artwork Description: Use watercolors to paint a dreamy and ethereal landscape. Let the colors blend and flow, creating a sense of magic and wonder. Add elements like shooting stars, a moonlit sky, or fantastical creatures to evoke a feeling of awe and mystery.

Concept: Peace Artwork Description: Create a tranquil scene using calming shades of blues and greens. Paint a serene landscape with a flowing river, gentle waves, or a peaceful meadow. Incorporate soft brushstrokes and use lighter shades to convey a sense of serenity and inner peace.

Concept: Dreams Artwork Description: Use mixed-media techniques to create a dream-inspired piece. Cut out silhouettes of dream-like objects such as clouds, stars, or butterflies from colored paper. Arrange them on a canvas or paper, and add splashes of pastel watercolors to create a whimsical and surreal atmosphere.

Encourage children to explore their creativity and experiment with different art materials and techniques to capture the ineffable essence of these concepts visually. Display their artworks proudly to celebrate their imaginative interpretations of the unexplainable.

The Ineffable Poetry Slam: Have children write short poems about their experiences of the ineffable. Encourage them to use descriptive language, metaphors, and vivid imagery to capture the essence of the unexplainable in their verses.

Here are some examples of short poems about the ineffable that children can write for The Ineffable Poetry Slam:

Poem: "Whispers of Wonder" In twilight's hush, I stand in awe, A world unseen, beyond my claw. Colors dance, like fireflies at night, My heart takes flight, in pure delight.

I chase the stars, their secrets untold, A universe of dreams, I behold. Words fail to capture what I see, The ineffable, forever free.

Poem: "The Song of Silence" In silence's embrace, I find, A language pure, beyond the mind. Like petals dancing in the breeze, The quiet whispers bring me peace.

A symphony of nothingness, Where time and space, they coalesce. The unspoken words, they say it all, The ineffable, in silence's thrall.

Poem: "Footsteps of Wonder" In fields of green, I take my stride, Where nature's magic cannot hide. The fragrance sweet, the flowers bloom, I find the ineffable in nature's room.

I follow paths of winding trees, They whisper secrets on the breeze. Through sunlit meadows, I explore, The unexplainable, forever more.

Poem: "Whirlwind of Dreams" I close my eyes and start to twirl, A whirlwind of dreams, a cosmic swirl. Colors blend, and stars align, The ineffable, in my mind's shrine.

I dance among the cosmic fire, A universe of infinite desire. With every step, my spirit soars, The unattainable, forever adored.

Poem: "A Canvas of Wonder" With brush in hand, I dip in dreams, Painting scenes of the unseen realms. Vivid hues and strokes untamed, The ineffable, forever framed.

My canvas sings with mystery, A world beyond our reality. Through colors bold and strokes divine, The unexplainable, in art we find.

Encourage children to let their imagination flow and express their own experiences and interpretations of the ineffable through their poetry.

The Ineffable Treasure Hunt: Hide small objects or pictures that represent ineffable concepts around the house or a designated play area. Provide children with clues or riddles that hint at the unexplainable nature of these concepts. Let them embark on a treasure hunt, searching for these symbolic representations of the ineffable.

Here are a few examples of clues or riddles that you can use to guide children on The Ineffable Treasure Hunt:

Clue: "I am everywhere, yet cannot be seen. I bring joy, sadness, and everything in between. Look for me where dreams take flight, where the stars shine bright at night." Symbol: A feather Explanation: The concept of emotions or feelings, which are intangible and can't be physically seen.

Clue: "I am a question without an answer, a mystery that lasts forever. Seek me out where knowledge lies, where the curious mind never dies." Symbol: A question mark Explanation: The concept of unanswered questions or the pursuit of knowledge.

Clue: "I am a whisper in the wind, a secret known to few. Find me in stories that unfold, where the characters come alive and take hold." Symbol: An open book Explanation: The concept of imagination or the power of storytelling.

Clue: "I am the spark that ignites the flame, the force that cannot be tamed. Seek me in the realm of creation, where ideas take shape and reach elation." Symbol: A paintbrush Explanation: The concept of creativity or the act of bringing something new into existence.

Clue: "I am the bridge between worlds unseen, the unbreakable bond that lies between. Look for me where friendship grows, where hearts connect and love flows." Symbol: A puzzle piece Explanation: The concept of connection or the importance of relationships.

Clue: "I am a melody without words, a language understood by all. Search for me where music resides, where harmony dances and joy abides." Symbol: A musical note Explanation: The concept of music or the power of sound to evoke emotions.

Feel free to adapt these examples or create your own clues and symbols based on the ineffable concepts you want to introduce to the children. Happy treasure hunting!

The Ineffable Journal: Encourage children to keep a journal where they can record moments, thoughts, or experiences that they find difficult to put into words. They can use drawings, symbols, or even invent their own language to capture the essence of the ineffable.

Here are some examples of how children can capture the essence of the ineffable in their journal:

Moment: Watching the Sunrise Description: Draw a vibrant orange and pink sky with the sun rising over the horizon. Use soft brushstrokes or colored pencils to create a gentle and serene atmosphere. Add a few words or symbols to convey the feeling of awe and wonder experienced during this ineffable moment.

Thought: Loss and Healing Description: Create a visual representation of emotions related to loss and healing. Draw a broken heart mending itself, with delicate lines and intricate patterns showing the process of healing. Use contrasting colors to represent the mix of sadness and hope, and add any symbols or words that resonate with your personal journey.

Experience: Being in Nature Description: Use colored pencils or watercolors to depict a lush, green forest with tall trees, birds, and flowing water. Capture the essence of the experience with detailed textures and vibrant colors. Add symbols like a smiling sun or a pair of hiking boots to represent the feelings of peace, connection, and awe that come with being in nature.

Moment: Laughter with Friends Description: Draw a group of friends with big smiles on their faces, laughing and having a joyful time. Use bright and warm colors to convey the happiness and energy of the moment. Add symbols like musical notes or exaggerated motion lines to express the contagious nature of laughter and the ineffable joy it brings.

Thought: Dreams and Imagination Description: Create a collage using magazine cutouts, colored paper, and your own drawings to represent the realm of dreams and imagination. Combine fantastical elements like flying unicorns, castles in the clouds, or floating islands. Use colors and shapes that evoke a sense of magic and wonder, capturing the ineffable nature of dreams.

Encourage children to explore different artistic techniques and materials, as well as their own invented symbols or language, to express the ineffable in their journal. This allows them to tap into their creativity and reflect on moments and experiences that may be difficult to put into words alone.

The Ineffable Reflection Circle: Gather children in a circle and take turns sharing experiences or moments that left them in awe or wonder. Encourage them to describe the ineffable aspects of these experiences and how they felt in those moments. Foster a supportive and respectful environment where children can freely express their thoughts and emotions.

Here are some examples of experiences or moments that children can share in The Ineffable Reflection Circle:

Experience: Stargazing on a Clear Night
Description: "I remember lying on a blanket and looking up at the night sky. There were so many stars, and it felt like I was part of something bigger. It was hard to put into words how beautiful and vast the universe seemed. I felt so small yet connected to everything at the same time."

Moment: Witnessing a Rainbow after a Storm
Description: "After a heavy rain shower, I saw a rainbow appear in the sky. The colors were so vivid and magical. It was like a bridge between the sky and the earth. I couldn't fully

explain the feeling of joy and hope that washed over me. It was like a gift from nature."

Experience: Exploring a Hidden Waterfall Description: "I stumbled upon a hidden waterfall while hiking. The sound of rushing water and the mist in the air created a sense of wonder. I stood there, feeling so alive and amazed by the beauty of nature. It was an experience that words couldn't capture, but I knew it was something special."

Moment: Holding a Newborn Baby Description: "When I held my baby sister for the first time, I felt an indescribable mix of emotions. She was so small and fragile, yet filled with potential. It was as if I was witnessing the miracle of life unfolding right before my eyes. I couldn't find the words to express the overwhelming love and awe I felt."

Experience: Watching a Thunderstorm from a Safe Place Description: "During a thunderstorm, I found shelter and watched the lightning streak across the sky and listened to the rumble of thunder. It was both thrilling and humbling. The power of nature was awe-inspiring, and it made me realize how grand

and uncontrollable the world can be. It was an ineffable experience that left me in awe."

Create a safe and respectful environment for children to share their reflections. Encourage active listening and empathy among participants, allowing them to appreciate each other's unique perspectives on the ineffable aspects of their experiences.

The Ineffable Nature Walk: Take children on a nature walk and encourage them to observe the beauty and intricacies of the natural world. As they explore, ask them to identify and discuss the aspects that feel ineffable or defy easy explanation. Encourage them to use their senses to connect with the unexplainable wonders of nature.

Here are some examples of aspects of nature that children can observe and discuss during The Ineffable Nature Walk:

Observation: A Butterfly's Dance Description: "Look at the butterfly gracefully fluttering from flower to flower. Its delicate wings seem to carry it effortlessly through the air. It's fascinating how such a small creature can bring so much joy and wonder. The way it moves is ineffable, as if it holds a secret connection to the breeze itself."

Observation: Sunlight Filtering Through Leaves Description: "Notice how the sunlight filters through the leaves of the trees, creating a beautiful dappled effect on the ground. It's as if nature is painting with light. The patterns and shadows are mesmerizing and difficult to put into words. It feels like stepping into a magical realm where the ordinary becomes extraordinary."

Observation: Sound of a Babbling Brook Description: "Listen to the soothing sound of the babbling brook nearby. The water flowing over rocks and the gentle gurgling create a peaceful melody. It's hard to describe how this sound makes me feel, but it's as if it washes away any worries and brings a sense of calm and serenity."

Observation: A Majestic Mountain Range Description: "Look at the vast mountain range in the distance, with its peaks touching the sky. The grandeur and magnificence are overwhelming. It's difficult to grasp the sheer size and power of these mountains, reminding us of the immensity of nature and our place in the world. It's an ineffable sight that fills me with awe."

Observation: Fragrance of Blooming Flowers Description: "Take a deep breath and smell the sweet fragrance of the blooming flowers around us. Each flower has its unique scent that fills the air. It's amazing how a scent can evoke memories and emotions, taking us to places beyond the physical world. The scent of these flowers is truly ineffable."

Encourage children to engage all their senses during the nature walk and express their observations using descriptive language. Encourage discussions about the unexplainable aspects of nature and allow them to explore their own interpretations of the wonders they encounter. The goal is to foster a deeper connection with nature and an appreciation for the ineffable beauty that surrounds us.

The Ineffable Collaborative Art Project: Divide children into small groups and provide each group with a large canvas or poster board. Ask them to work together to create a collaborative artwork that represents the ineffable. Encourage them to incorporate different artistic techniques and materials to capture the essence of the unexplainable as a collective expression.

Here are some examples of collaborative art projects that children can create to represent the ineffable:

Project: "Unseen Connections" Description: Instruct each group to create a large interconnected web on the canvas using colorful threads or yarn. Let the threads represent the invisible connections that exist between people, nature, and the universe. Encourage the children to add drawings or symbols along the threads to represent different aspects of the ineffable that they feel connected to.

Project: "Beyond Words" Description: Ask each group to paint a vibrant and abstract background on the canvas, using bold brushstrokes and expressive colors. Then, provide them with magazines, newspapers, and other print materials. Instruct the children to cut out words, phrases, and images that represent the ineffable to them and collages them onto the painted background, creating a layered and textured composition.

Project: "Rhythms of the Unseen" Description: Have each group use a combination of paint, pastels, and markers to create a rhythmic and flowing abstract artwork. Encourage them to layer different patterns, lines, and shapes to represent the intangible and unexplainable energies that exist in the world. Add metallic or iridescent materials to enhance the sense of mystery and wonder.

Project: "Embracing the Unknown" Description: Provide each group with a large canvas and ask them to create a mixed media collage. Instruct them to use a variety of materials such as fabric scraps, natural objects, feathers, and found objects to create a textured and layered artwork. Encourage them to incorporate elements that symbolize the ineffable, such as open doors, puzzle pieces, or mystical creatures.

Project: "Uncharted Territories" Description:
Assign each group a specific color palette and
ask them to collaboratively paint a large map-
like artwork on the canvas. Encourage them to
incorporate abstract shapes, symbols, and
intricate patterns to represent the unexplored
territories of the ineffable. They can also add
elements of nature, dreams, and imagination
to the map to reflect the sense of wonder and
possibility.

Encourage children to work together, share
ideas, and respect each other's contributions
during the collaborative art project. The goal is
to create a collective representation of the
ineffable that combines different perspectives
and artistic techniques.

By engaging in these fun games, children can
continue to explore and deepen their
understanding of the ineffable. They can
embrace the joy of creative expression,
expand their imaginations, and nurture their
sense of wonder. These activities will
encourage children to think beyond words and
tap into the unexplainable aspects of life,
fostering a lifelong appreciation for the

mysteries and beauty that exist beyond what can be easily articulated.

Other books to develop the children's exploration of the unknown, the unseen, the spiritual, the incomprehensible and who they really are on this 3d Dimension and ascending towards 5th.

Inner Senses Amazon ASIN # B0C9X733L3

Spiritual yoga Amazon ASIN # B082FP5YS8

Source of Being Amazon ASIN # B08Y7YC843

A course in miracles for children ACIM Amazon ASIN # B0BXL719KR

Paul Ardennes

Researcher in Energy fields

Paul Ardennes is an Author. He is working with various publishers including *Amazon* and *Barnes & Noble*. He is retired from active life.

He also publishes on educational platforms such as *Udemy & Simpliv on **Spiritual Yoga***.

He is a trained Electronic Medicine practitioner (Scenar Cosmodic, Auricular therapy, Meridian Imaging charting, electronic iris analysis, laser therapy and so on...), and **an energy healer** (Seichim and Usui Reiki Master, informational medicine). He still helps people for free. His wife is a Doctor Gynaecologist from Ukraine and a keen supporter of his work.

He developed his energy research interest when he visited the De la Warr Radionics Laboratories in Oxford, UK in the 80s. They are now closed due to lack of research funding.

Amazon Editorial Team

I dedicate this book to Lucy, the Galactic Light who found me, and now disappears when I appear. *Bonsoir Galucya.*

Serge

Printed in Great Britain
by Amazon

33280346R00037